SCIENCE MEASUREMENTS

How Heavy? How Long? How Hot?

by Chris Eboch   illustrated by Jon Davis

PICTURE WINDOW BOOKS
Minneapolis, Minnesota

Thanks to our advisers for their expertise, research, and advice:

Jeffrey R. Pribyl, Ph.D.
Professor of Chemistry and Geology
Minnesota State University, Mankato

Susan Kesselring, M.A., Literacy Educator
Rosemount–Apple Valley–Eagan (Minnesota) School District

Editors: Jacqueline Wolfe and Nick Healy
Designer: Ben White
Page Production: Joseph Anderson
Creative Director: Keith Griffin
Editorial Director: Carol Jones
The illustrations in this book were created digitally.

This book was produced for Picture Window Books by
Bender Richardson White, U.K.

Picture Window Books
5115 Excelsior Boulevard
Suite 232
Minneapolis, MN 55416
877-845-8392
www.picturewindowbooks.com

Printed in the United States of America.

Library of Congress Cataloging-in-Publication Data
Eboch, Chris.
Science measurements : how heavy?, how long?, how hot? /
by Chris Eboch; illustrated by Jon Davis.
p. cm. — (Amazing science)
Includes biographical references and index.
ISBN-13: 978-1-4048-2197-2 (hardcover)
ISBN-10: 1-4048-2197-X (hardcover)
1. Physical measurements—Juvenile literature. I. Davis, Jon, ill.
II. Title. III. Series.
QC39.5.E36 2007
530.8—dc22   2006008321

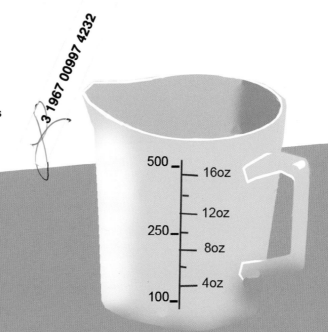

Table of Contents

Measuring the World

Scientists study how the world works. They find out when, where, and why things happen. To do that, they need to keep track of exactly what they observe. They need to make good measurements.

Measuring uses numbers to describe something. How big is it? How heavy is it? How hot is it? Has it changed since the last time it was measured?

You, too, can measure things. Let's try baking some cookies. You'll see how you need measurements even when you do something fun.

FUN FACT

Most Americans use English measurements, such as inches and pounds. The metric system is used in many other countries.

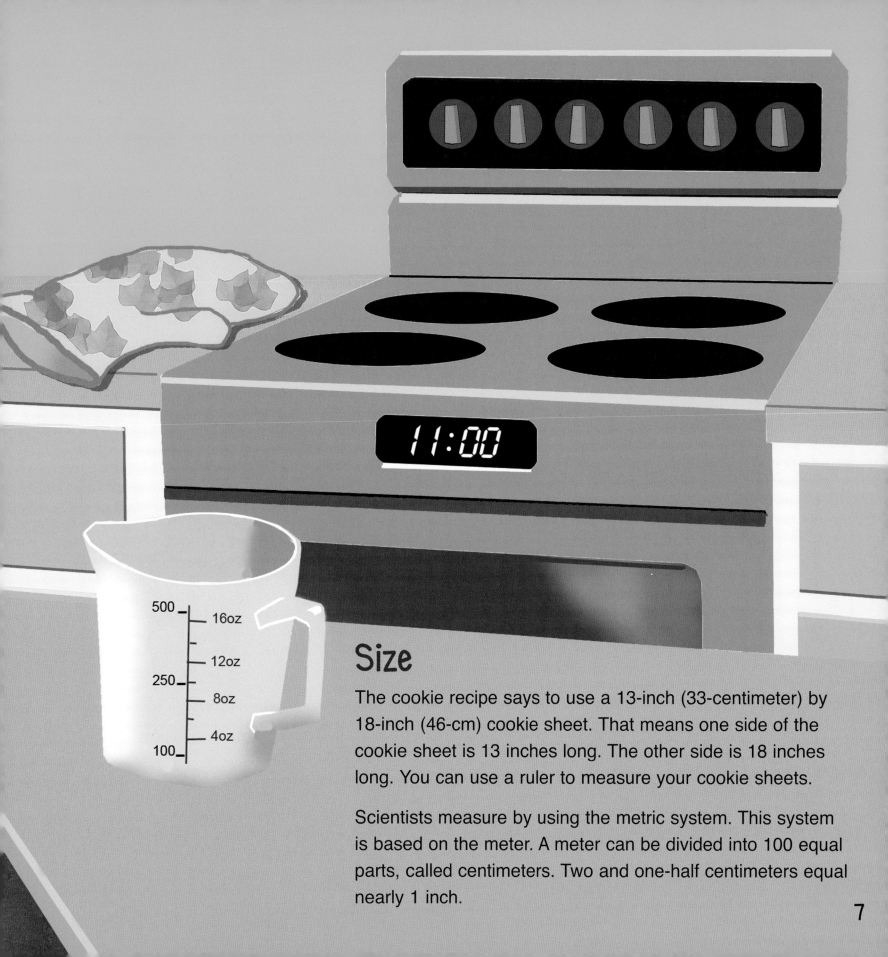

Size

The cookie recipe says to use a 13-inch (33-centimeter) by 18-inch (46-cm) cookie sheet. That means one side of the cookie sheet is 13 inches long. The other side is 18 inches long. You can use a ruler to measure your cookie sheets.

Scientists measure by using the metric system. This system is based on the meter. A meter can be divided into 100 equal parts, called centimeters. Two and one-half centimeters equal nearly 1 inch.

7

Volume

To make cookies, you need ingredients such as eggs and sugar. It's easy to count eggs, but how do you measure sugar? You can't count every grain. You can't measure how long it is, either.

You need to measure the volume of the sugar. Volume measures how much space something takes up. We use measuring cups to measure volume. The recipe will tell you how many cups (or metric milliliters) of flour and sugar you need.

FUN FACT
Some things can change volume. Water fills more space as it freezes. Don't put a full plastic bottle of water in the freezer. The water will expand and break the bottle.

9

Small Measurements

Cookies need only a little bit of salt. It's easier to measure a small amount with measuring spoons. They measure parts of a cup. These parts are called teaspoons and tablespoons. The metric system uses milliliters to measure smaller volumes.

Scientists also measure volume with the metric system. They have measuring cups and beakers marked in liters and milliliters.

Everything is made up of matter. Matter can be solid, like a brick. It can be liquid, like milk. It can be a gas, like air. We usually measure the size of a solid. We usually measure the volume of a liquid or gas.

11

Temperature

The ingredients have been measured and mixed. Now it is time to bake the cookies. The oven must be set at the right temperature. Temperature measures how hot or cold something is.

Americans use the Fahrenheit scale to measure temperatures. People in many other countries use the Celsius scale to measure temperatures. Scientists also use the Celsius scale.

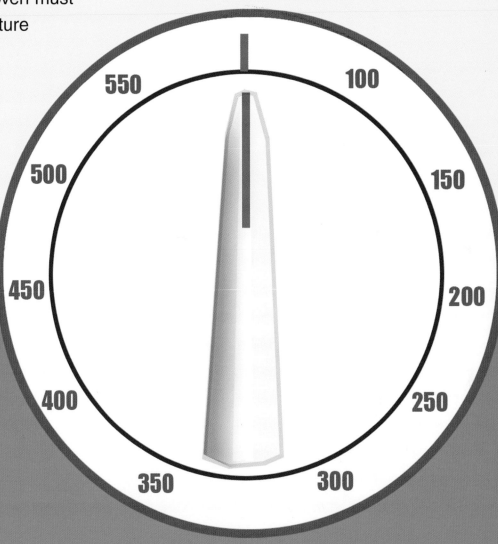

FUN FACT

The hottest outdoor temperature ever recorded was in the country of Libya in Africa. The air was 136 degrees Fahrenheit (58 degrees Celsius) in the shade.

Hot and Cold

We measure temperature in many ways in daily life. Water boils at 212° F. Water freezes at 32° F. In most places, outside temperatures are usually between 0° F and 100° F. Cookies usually bake at 350° F.

Scientists often use the Celsius scale to measure temperature. Water boils at 100° C. Water freezes at 0° C. In most places, outside temperatures are usually between minus 18° C and 38° C. Cookies usually bake at 177° C.

FUN FACT
The coldest outdoor temperature ever recorded
was minus 129° F (minus 89° C) in Antarctica.

Time

Cookies bake in the oven. You must bake them for the right amount of time, and you can use a timer to keep track of time. The timer rings a bell or buzzer when time is up.

Scientists sometimes have to measure very small amounts of time. Minutes are not small enough. Seconds are not small enough. Scientists use a special atomic clock to measure a tiny part of a second.

A clock measures the passing of time in minutes and hours. A calendar also measures time. It measures days, weeks, months, and years. One year is the time it takes Earth to revolve around the sun.

Weight

Scientists use scales in their laboratories. A scale measures how heavy things are. Scientists often weigh things by using the metric system, which measures weight in grams.

Sometimes cooks measure ingredients by weight instead of by volume. A cooking scale may be marked in ounces or grams. Sixteen ounces (456 grams) make 1 pound.

18

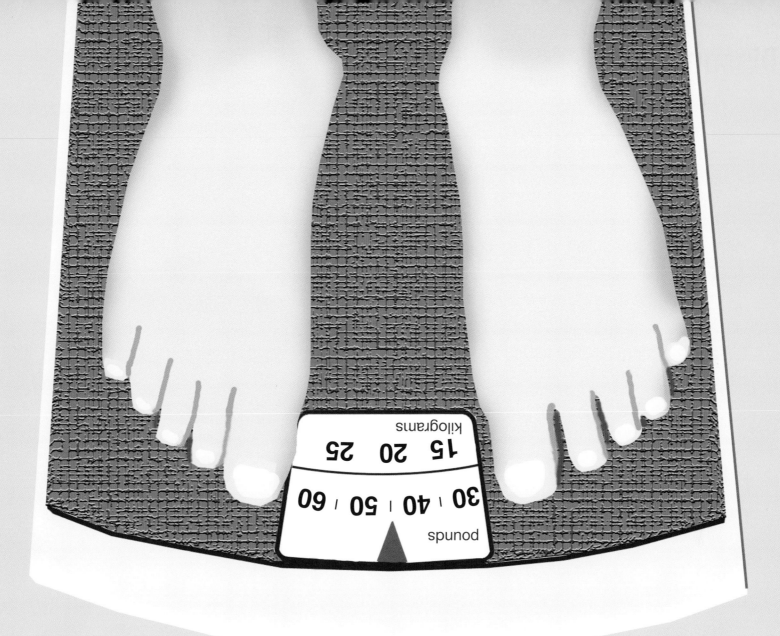

FUN FACT

Many people have scales in their homes so they can weigh themselves. We measure our weight in pounds or kilograms.

Distance

Take some cookies to school. How far do you travel to get there? Inches and feet work well for measuring small distances. For a longer distance, you may want to use miles. One mile is 5,280 feet. The metric system measures length with the meter. For long distances, it uses kilometers. A kilometer is 1,000 meters. It takes 1.6 kilometers to make 1 mile.

While sharing your cookies, you might think about the many measurements we used to make them. We measured the size of the cookie sheet and the volume of the ingredients. We also measured the temperature in the oven and the time needed for baking. We even measured the distance to bring our treat to friends. Careful measurements helped us do the job right.

FUN FACT

Scientists who study space measure distance in light-years. A light-year is the distance light travels in one year. Nothing can travel faster than light. The closest star is more than four light-years away from Earth.

21

Chocolate Chip Cookies

What you need:

8 ounces (224 g) butter, softened

1 cup (240 mL) sugar

1/2 cup (120 mL) brown sugar

2 eggs

2 teaspoons (10 mL) vanilla

2 1/2 cups (60 mL) flour

1 teaspoon (5 mL) baking soda

1 teaspoon (5 mL) salt

12 ounces (336 g) chocolate chips

electric mixer and large mixing bowl

cookie sheet

measuring cups and spoons

mixing spoon

What you do:

1. Preheat the oven temperature to 350° F (177° C).
2. Put the butter, sugar, and brown sugar in a large bowl. Mix them together until smooth. Ask an adult to use an electric mixer for this task.
3. Add the eggs and vanilla to the bowl. Stir well.
4. Put the flour, baking soda, and salt in another bowl. Stir them together.
5. Blend the flour mixture into the first bowl. Stir in the chocolate chips.
6. Shape large spoonfuls of cookie dough (about 2 tablespoons or 30 mL of dough) into balls. Leave an even amount of space between the balls of dough on the cookie sheet. You should be able to fit about 12 cookies on the sheet.
7. Have an adult put the sheet in the oven.
8. Set a timer for 10 minutes. When the timer goes off, have an adult check the cookies. They should be light brown but still soft in the center. If they are not quite done, bake for one or two more minutes.
9. When the cookies are done, have an adult take the pan from the oven. Let the cookies cool on the pan for one or two minutes. Have the adult move the cookies to a wire rack to finish cooling.
10. Put more balls of cookie dough on the sheet and bake them. Keep doing this until all the batter has been used.

Science Measurements Extras

Big Feet?

Most Americans measure length in inches and feet. A long time ago, an inch was thought to be the width of a person's thumb. A foot was the length of a person's foot. This wasn't a good form of measurement. Why not? Different people had thumbs and feet of very different sizes.

The Best Yard

For longer measurements, we use yardsticks. A yard is 3 feet (0.9 m). A standard yard is kept in a special vault in London. This stick is made of metal. All other yardsticks must be the same size as that standard yard.

The Size of Weight

Which is heavier, 1 pound (0.45 kilogram) of feathers or 1 pound (0.45 kg) of lead? They weigh the same, of course: 1 pound. But the pound of feathers will take up a lot more space than the pound of lead. It has a bigger volume.

How Hot Are You?

You can use a thermometer to check your own temperature. The temperature inside your body should be about 98.6° F (37° C). A higher body temperature probably means you are sick.

Glossary

beakers—glass or plastic cups and tubes used to hold liquids

matter—anything that takes up space

metric system—a system of measurement based on groups of 10

ounce—a unit of weight (1/16 of a pound or 28 g) or volume (1/8 of a cup or 30 mL)

revolve—to turn or to circle around another object

temperature—hotness or coldness

thermometer—a tool used to measure temperature

volume—how much space something takes up

weight—how heavy something is

To Learn More

At the Library

Kensler, Chris. *Secret Treasures and Magical Measures Revealed.* New York: Simon and Schuster, 2003.

Sargent, Brian. *How Heavy Is It?* New York: Children's Press, 2005.

Schwartz, David M. *Millions to Measure.* New York: HarperCollins, 2003.

Sweeney, Joan. *Me and the Measure of Things.* New York: Crown Publishers, 2001.

On the Web

FactHound offers a safe, fun way to find Internet sites related to this book. All of the sites on FactHound have been researched by our staff.

1. Visit *www.facthound.com*
2. Type in this special code for age-appropriate sites: 140482197X
3. Click on the FETCH IT button.

Your trusty FactHound will fetch the best sites for you!

Look for other books in the Amazing Science series:

Composting: Nature's Recyclers
   1-4048-2194-5
Erosion: Changing Earth's Surface
   1-4048-2195-3
Magnification: A Closer Look
   1-4048-2196-1
Science Safety: Being Careful
   1-4048-2198-8
Science Tools:
   Using Machines and Instruments
   1-4048-2199-6